Other Books by Jared Smith:

Poetry:

Song of the Blood: An Epic
Dark Wing
Keeping the Outlaw Alive
Walking the Perimeters of the Plate Glass Window Factory

Technology:

Introducing Personal Computer Use in the Gas Industry (Bukacek. Smith, eds.)
Integrating Microelectronics Into Gas Distribution (Rush, Huebler, Smith, eds.)
Gas, Oil, and Coal Biotechnology (Akin, Smith, eds.)

LAKE MICHIGAN
and Other Poems

By Jared Smith

The Puddin'head Press
2005

Additional copies of this book
may be ordered by writing to:

The Puddin'head Press
PO Box 477889
Chicago IL 60647
708-656-4900

www.puddinheadpress.com

Cover photograph by David Lightner
Author photograph by Charlie Rossiter

First Edition
2005

ISBN# 978-0-9724339-4-5

Dedication:

Dedicated to:
Deborah Parriott Smith

Acknowledgements

Some poems in this collection previously appeared in the following locations:

"Finding Oneself in an American Fairytale" appeared in *Juice*.

"Eyes" and "When It's Time To Go" appeared in *Spoon River Poetry Review*.

"Lake Michigan" first appeared in *After Hours*, and was been adapted to stage under the title *Jared Smith's 'Lake Michigan'* for a 2004 opening in Chicago.

"Things to Remember," and "Of Moons" appeared in *The Greenfield Review*

"Returning Home" appeared in *Crosscountry*

"Passage From Home" and "Mood In Grays" appeared in *Dacotah Territory*

"An Erosion" appeared in *U.T. Review*

"Erie" appeared in *Illinois Review*

"Talking To My Son" appeared in *The New York Quarterly*

"Controlled by Ghosts" has appeared in *Trail & Timberline* and at *ChicagoPoets.com*

"Seven Minutes Before The Bombs Drop" has appeared in *After Hours* and at *poetrypoetry.com*, linked to *Poets Against the War*.

"Coming of Age" appeared in *DuPage Literary Arts Journal*.

"Getting Ready to Move On," "Tossing Jobs Around Like Manhole Covers," and "When All is Said" appeared first at *ChicagoPoets.com*

Table of Contents

"God is that than which nothing greater can be conceived.
    --Anselm

What have we seen beyond our sunset fires
That lights again the way by which we came?
    --Edwin Arlington Robinson

LAKE MICHIGAN
And Other Poems

By Jared Smith

Getting Ready To Move On

The last flowers blaze their dry color
like Easter baskets left outside all year into the first freeze of autumn,
their reds and oranges flaming from dry frost-bit stalks.
This is the last day after sixteen years we will tend them.
In the spring rains, a new enormous house of fieldstone
will fill this garden with its family of four and three car garage.
This is the garden that glowed the golden color of my wife's hair,
gone cold now with memory and the need to be elsewhere.

We will not be here,
having followed the leaves in their last ecstasy,
The empty rooms of our children will have been torn down:
our children will be lying with their own in other beds.
They will come and go with the turning of books in far away towns.

I think, if we are lucky, the photographs from inside our house
will be carried on a coyote's wail into the night of western mountains.
There will be parties by candlelight on desert slopes with desert friends.
There will be winter streams that lay a black ice over these years
so that we can skate over them dancing above our aging friends.
If we are lucky, there will be no pain in letting go.

Passage From Home

Far down   where the road went out to dust
flickers rose in thickets from our tires.
And that was where the girls went for their first affairs
   with rock
   with the waters
where their dry casings afterward rattled the earth
   as locust wings;
but also where they learned to grow eyes for seeing in the night.
There.   Here
where the office buildings now stand
row upon circling row
forming natural arenas for the strips of meadowgrass.
There is something sad about this town—
in the ease with which it perches in expectation
   of the coming boom
even when no children return at night to drink their milk before the fire.

A little town
formed of the webs of young thought
and abandoned in the granite of time;
a flat stretch beneath the volcanic columns of cumulous clouds
which hold the light for many hours
after the evening news is first turned on.

Mood In Grays

Snow fell last night
burrowing through the minds of white moths
whose crackled legs spring the shortness of lifespans.

The sighs of the unfed
who turn down the liquid throat of dreams
having never been conceived
half-haunt the recorder taking notes
of blackbird shadows among the first reeds of day.

The turbulence of the father's oak
planted thirty years before earth took shape
prime-moves the cattle going home...
flicking ambitions in a dead man's skull
paving the way of forgotten trails.

Lake Michigan

Understanding   Lake Michigan
    is like shoving a small straw into the nozzle of a fire hose
& sucking while someone turns the pressure up...
Twenty-two thousand square miles of surface pressure/
forty-five thousand four hundred and ten roughly if you include the Huron lobe
narrowing down to between three and five miles in the Mackinac Straits
                     --not that narrow even then
to be going through a straw and out through the back of your head;
              very few
that's like understanding Lake Michigan through a strand of neurons.
It's like broadband when you've got a phone modem stuck in your head.

                              Heavy, rusting lake to lake freighters
                   carrying dark-grained earth metals from the north country
                       and light-grained earth grains from the east country
                           down to the southern lake steel mills
                swirling among each other and some of them catching out
                     into the chain of water narrowing to the St. Lawrence
                        where they exchange cargo with the ocean freighters
                going off to Europe or north or down along the southern coast...
                           deep rusting corridors of time containing life.

Try telling *that* Lake Michigan to the young stud selling *Streetwise* on the corner.
Try telling *that* to the businessman you meet from out of town;
it's not something you can put into everyday conversation.
I mean, it's big...
this thing that caused all the eastward bound limestone and iron ore
to back up against it and rise up into piles of office buildings.

Where the wind blows it is cold and dangerous,
and your hands bleed as they grab wet metal, cold, feeling nothing.
You are a wraith of oilskin plastic held by knotted hemp in the constant gale
and the buildings so close on shore and the eyes from the offices on shore
cannot reach you as the waters roil about your feet
off Milwaukee Chicago Gary
it is night
and the dark is pierced with stars and corporate windows.

It ought to come through eventually though,
   maybe intimate talk like late at night,
us being ninety-eight per cent water,
it sure as heck ought to come through for us in Chicago
                awash in this
drawing our drinking water from the Lake,
that what comes into us is what thinks about what comes in…
is The Muskegon, Grand, Kalamazoo, Fox, and Menominee Rivers
   along with all their fish and plant life
            and human sweat
in the form of sulfur, coal dust, mercury & heavy metals,
   pesticides, fertilizers
and, well, fertilizers among other things we hold close.

Curse and sing in the wind
as you batten the hatches, you lords of Lake Michigan.
Your flesh will be battered as the rocky basin itself
and your lungs filled with icy cold 'til they can take no more…
then only you will fly as angels.

A great blue heron fishes the Calumet.
It wades among a vertical landscape of greens.
Its sleek gray plumage towers over its domain,
and it picks from among the schools of fish
                drawn to its shadow for shelter
so quickly that nothing is disturbed.

What comes into us in Chicago
comes down from the cold north woods as well,
from ground springs drawn from aquifers with hundred year retentions,
                sea of experience
from among the deep roots of hidden pines on unsold acreage,
swirling down along the whole western flank, stopping by Milwaukee and Green Bay,
fingering and then bulling its way through the impediments we've built up
                working at undercutting and filling in our built-in swamps
        and swirling itself out into arid dunes if it misses the city
and gets past the Calumet and other manmade harbors to the south
it hooks back up for another pass or it goes down inside itself.

                Eyes bloody, faces creased with time and sun
        invisible in the nighttime until you have led the way and lit the lights,
                        your clothing hanging in shrouds
                your face looking upward from unclear distance
                        and your lips silent and gone.

        Sitting around the table, thirty men from U of C
        are compiling data sheets on their PCs.
        "You can get ten cars per interval node
        through this sector across this stretch of road

block by block across the country." And NOAA,
and EPA doing the same trick by cubic feet of lake
compile the same to see what they can make
when data is combined and you have a map.
PCs to PCs data tap data tap data tap.
"I think I can see what we have here, " says one.
"What can we sell it for? "
Hey, it's a life.

This thing is so big that when it breathes
                    are accorded
we reshape the city.
When it goes down in drought every heavy freighter on the lake
unloads 350 tons of cargo for every inch the water goes down to remain afloat;
now when you're talking ten year drought that's a heap of jobs per inch
trickling out everywhere from the western quarries and mines
    to those rip-rap towers of glass along LaSalle
        to industrial centers in Germany and England or France
maybe nine or ten thousand tons per trip per ship lost when the rain don't fall,
and when you're talking heavy rains and heavy winter snow cycles
    then you're talking about giving land away because we build too close.

                                saying something startling new
                    about the young laughter in bar rooms and casual getting to know
                                that goes on beneath bitter nights torn with rage.
                                    And you will succeed
                        you will in this city that comes from the earth
                            as much as the stars are from the earth
                            and as distant as thought reflecting off water

Either way, it's high cost maintenance
    and it's in Chicago's bones…
this thing that came out of the last ice age
                    the opportunity
left by something massive slouching down from the Arctic,
something like nothing else in all the world to fill the arteries of Chicago brawlers.
It takes a pig-headed fool, a hog butcher with a penchant for getting into fights
and a delight in coming out even, but with new adrenaline in the blood;
It takes that Captain-of-the-Plains mentality to belly up to the bar here,
to recreate the grandeur of the glaciers and walk among them,
to reflect back the jagged ice flows of winter stacked up along the outer drive,
to grapple with this thing in all its seasons and take life deep.

                    sometimes lightly as a sandpiper darting along the shore
                scrutinizing patterns in the way sand is piled on pebbles and
                    grasping life from what is tossed upward by the elements

                From the Hancock observation deck
                cars disappear into your shadow.
                They do not have anything to do with you.
                You yourself are as tall as anything on the lake,
                and you are blind in the early morning sunlight.
                Nothing is disturbed.

It's a fang-toothed, snarling monster of an idea too,
this idea of ever making partnership with such an ancient relic.
Hard to think about while clinking your ice cubes together in The Prairie Restaurant,
                    to reflect

but this lake has pulled the life from more men and women in Chicago
than any other natural force; and we keep on coming back like we need a fight
whether relishing the crafty hidden power of lights along the lake
        on a midnight cruise celebrating prom night
           or a sales meeting success night
              or a dinner with the out-of-towners
knowing that this is not something that will last unless we take it in/

or whether meeting the gales of trade straight on where cargoes shift and ships go down.
Seventy thousand tons of cargo shifting is a lot to think about,
and it's something makes a man learn to do his job carefully in the heartland.

              sometimes a shear dress clinging to young hips
         pressed across a taut belly bearing an impossibly young birth
            with the sun setting just right along the shore...
           and she with her lips parted and moving silently
        so that you could almost hear them if you bedded her.

I mean, this thing is big.
It brought the steel mills to the heartland.
You could see the train cars pulled up by the steel mills
waiting for the men inside to finish pounding out long ribbons of steel into bands
that wound back and forth across the factory floor curled around supporting posts with
the heat roaring off it and the ribbon just flowing along except when it got
caught on something
and then go snapping off the supporting posts and I swear those workers would
     jump
straight up high as their knees without pausing to think about it because
if you didn't, you lost your legs cut clean off

and everyone knew this
and it was part of life
until the whistle blew and then everyone would take his lunch pail and head for home
but lining out squeezed against the factory wall outside
                    on the experience
because that white hot steel gave off so much heat still when it was piled onto the trains.
Talk about *Rust Belt?* To Hell with MBAs; it built America!!

                    But either way or in whatever image before culmination it gets
                              pulled away beneath your feet
                         and you are standing as if on air, the cold
                    thrill filling you and your framework your understanding
                              filling with the cold waters of time. This
                    is how you learn to work quickly and surely, Chicago man.

                    Honey, what are *you* looking at?
                    This is the third place I've been in tonight.
                    Last week I was looking at the museums.
                    I've been to the cafes. I'm always looking.
                    I've tried a few on too, let me tell you,
                    but I know what I'm looking for…
                    cool, hard as thunder…gray as night,
                    I know what I'm looking for.

You can still find those steel bars in every industrial nation in the world;
You can find American specified steel piping under every American city built
   beyond the best specs. Washington or New York ever asked for,
bringing oil, and water, and natural gas and industry to every city.

And you can find those steel bars at the bottom of Lake Michigan as well.
It's not your garden variety pond.
It is a deep body of water, and that means it rolls over every year;
as the seasons change, the cold ice water from the surface swirls down
and the dead debris from the bottom rises on an anaerobic cloud
while the bright, living water drives downward nine hundred twenty-three feet,
    scouring around the bottom
        swirling nutrients into the mix
      washing along the ragged boards of ships sunk long ago.
It's not so far, not too deep to go, to travel back two hundred years in time
to probe among the wreckage of commerce long forgotten...
               they are participating in
to rise back and drop down again along a clear-lit tunnel of time
where the living and the dead pass constantly in this tunnel in the Midwest,
dancing past each other repeatedly as the seasons change.
The Lake itself can chill its surface 15 degrees Centigrade within 3 hours,
bringing with it whatever has lain upon the bottom until its time has come.
These are where the storm beaten boats went down, where it is deep.
In shoals, where glaciers left their jagged boulders
are other ships with cargoes of death, reaching out to snare pleasure craft;
sometimes a fisherman's line hung with Christmas trees for salmon will catch,
and a dead man's fingers will hang on for a moment saying *come back*
Come back; all things are as they ever were and there is peace within the lake.
Things have not changed so much from when Marquette and Joliet were where you are.
A drop of water that enters the lake remains within it for 99 years before passing on.
All things are fluid here, no harsh banging upon the wind and rocks you know above;
just these cold dark caverns and their chandeliers of weed.
We will rise on silver wings in the spring, you and I.

                        Yeah,

                              this rocking and turning platform
                        with its impending life and street corner
                                          leading nowhere
                                           is pretty special
                                             is the focus
                                            you've got
                                           is a window
                               looking through time.

The natives used to scare deer into the open by setting fire to the prairie.
One whole side of the lake seemed to be in flame that ran
high as the head of my horse, according to one pioneer's journal.
It would blow in the wind and it was as if it were the wind.
I have never been so scared or so drawn to anything in all my miles.

The numbers begin to mean less than nothing;
the tonnage of water and facts to be more than unconnected.
It is a big lake,
but not too big to rise from within itself
and be drawn down into the cribs that line its shore,
to be pulled inward through rock tunnels to the Chicago underground.
This lake is a masterful arena for pitting man and woman against the elements,
                              before they are
for burying those that fail and forgetting those that win.
It is a lake without natural outlets,
a lake like the urn Grecian gods drank from that never emptied;
but every man and every woman in Chicago drinks from it.
Every man and every woman in Chicago carries the lake within them,
and every plant and blade of grass that draws its water from the lake

is likewise of the lake,
with a memory that has no memory
that can be seen.

The lake thinks with what is within you
and what is within you in greatest part, Chicago, is the lake.
It   is pretty big.
It reaches up to swirl the jet streams that whip above our continent,
deflecting them north or south around its borders:
look at those loops you see on the weather map each night!
It is at the end of *Tornado Alley*,
a wall that breaks the elements,
                    a part of
and it is in us all more than we have ever known.
It is a hungry, ragged beast
that glimmers blue on the horizon of the ordinary,
tying every man who lives along its borders
                    it.
to every other man by everything we carry deep inside.

Somewhere over 787 rectangular boxes
filled with glassy eyes that have gone water into water
and have taken bone into water into time
are located just offshore looking up
where the strongest swimmers swim
in the heartland
at the bottom.

Controlled By Ghosts

The snows came in early over Monarch this year;
cold right behind them, whittling away at the firewood.
I stacked it extra high this year, seeing how thick the fur grew on the fox,
for all the good that did because it's already smaller now than usual.
I dragged dead aspens down the hill and chopped them up, piled them up
as long as my heart could take it this year; just until one day when I said
that's enough; that'll do it now;
and I went blank deep down in my bones and went inside and lit a fire.

The snows came in early this year, though, even so,
and the cold; it was so cold. And the snow was so deep you couldn't get out,
you couldn't climb the hills after awhile even when the sun was out.
You couldn't climb the hills to pull down any more wood, even if you had the heart.
The woodpile just kept getting smaller one day's heat at a time.
And the wind, it just kept coming in through the chinks in the wall,
so I'd sit there at night burning as little wood as I could and huddled
until my mind started wandering and I'd think about you
I'd think about you and Pete going down to the store last winter,
his arm bringing you in under the wind when you turned the corner,
not that I could see that much up behind the aspens where I worked.

My whole life has been controlled by ghosts;
that's mostly what I think about as I take the last cord of wood, piece by piece,
take it in and pile it by the cast iron stove your Momma bought.
It was a Christmas present the year we built this house, black and hard,
sitting here in the middle of our home waiting for winter.
Well, it came, of course. It came early that year as well
but of course there was a thaw come February like there usually is.
Not this year, though, with the woodpile all but gone.
I saw Pete, I think, yesterday way down the road,
saw him walking almost lightly over the snow as if it wasn't deep at all,

standing near the corner where the two of you used to pause,
looking like he wasn't sure where he was meant to be going now.
Then gone, of course. I suppose I should have got more wood,
but I thought I'd got enough; always did before.
There's a first time always, I guess, the cold comes down
and stays around until it finds what it's looking for.

Seven Minutes Before The Bombs Drop

…Everyone still has names.
Sand is gritting against my eyes when the wind blows,
scraping counterpoint to the dry coughs of my son beyond the wall.
There is no medicine that will help this, I think,
but music is playing on a radio down the street.
Everyone I know will be gathering there:
we will barter for what we need; trade scraggly chickens or dates for shoes;
trade shoes for drinking water before the sun gets high.
I will seek medicine among my friends.

Seven minutes before the bombs drop
we are sitting in the dim lights of a church reading poetry
talking with words meant for little animals we might keep tethered
or lock into our kitchens so they will not soil the rugs while we sleep.
Between the words, though, we are talking of other things,
are bartering whether we will wear chains about our necks
or will make it into old age in one piece ourselves;
and we are reflecting on the words of other solitary thinkers
who talked of war while drinking cognac in bomb shelters in the blitz.

Seven minutes before the bombs drop
we are crying, running, our bladders filled,
our muscles quickening as never before in Kansas,
and we thump our open hands down on throbbing metal fuselage.
We throw ourselves into cylinders that have only one direction to go.
The painted gray of the runway trembles, breaks loose, and falls away;
becomes the endlessly wide sere blankness of the sea…and then light
will begin beneath our wings. Sand into sand and dust into dust.
Testosterone may be a great thing, but it does not last without love.

I am going to go home when this evening ends

and sit with my wife and children around the dinner table;
we will light candles as a centerpiece, and we will drink wine.
I will turn the CD player on low and listen to the ancient songs;
the songs that are no longer written, and will cry.
Yes, I'm going to go there down the highway in my '96 Lumina;
faster than I should, outside the law, but in my Lumina.
That's okay; you can come too. You come too; there is no guilt
in holding onto each other in our despair through the miles;
there is no guilt unless we ever re-elect the darkness that envelopes us.
We are the light, if only by the choice of fate and mystery of words.

Finding Oneself In An American Fairy Tale

An artist arch-backed to the room,
   flexing the flesh at the base of her spine, she twists subtly.
Gaunt street lamps glint through the gauze of her hair
and her lips part to speak of holy babies crawling in the alleys.
She croons to them, offers herself each evening,
for evenings are the times of native american fairy tales
as much as days are built of eurasian fantasies.

She is the girl who danced naked for boys even before reaching puberty,
whose eyes led them farther even than her gentle fingers could,
beckoning to wind-tossed prairies moist with april's yield;
yet she is supple only in the night,
for the day has caught her clutching at her pocketbook,
looking over her shoulder, doubting herself and her reservations.

She dreams and lights a candle,
and the candle is a coyote whose calls surround the city.
The ululations are stories of the earth mother and sky father,
of the happy turtle carrying the universe on its worn shell;
but they are tricks
she finds, waking to the crash of paul bunyon striding onto fifth avenue,
and the blue sky is the blue eyes of his babe dumb-faced over an empty land.

She would stop johnny appleseed in his tracks even now,
but she is an artist and impales herself upon him
taking him deeply so that the urgency of her body transforms his seeds
and their steel skeletons twist and groan in the wind as they grow.

A Quantum Species

Life is that brief
multiple point in the cosmos
where entropy and energy reverse themselves
in contemplation,
a blemish on a gray monotony.

All that matters
agglomerates.
A woman in red blouse/black slacks
passes suddenly between a light and her wall
is reflected
through the web I detect motion within all my molecules.
Her message is on the night as it passes into electrodes.

I am a spider
tending its net between the stars,
a quantum species seeking for security.

In Our Attraction To Electronic Media

We are dark in the heart of stone,
but one flint of light is enough to give you air.
You draw the air from that light and put it out.
You are alone.
The moon is rising above you
over a deserted field of dried grass
and the air is dark and cold.
You light a match
and the dry grass catches hold.
You are a fire lifting the dry life around you,
and are drawn yourself to the fire.

When I call you on the telephone, I am reaching out and stroking
your flesh with my mind. But I see the telephone I call from,
perched on its white plastic end table, rather than the muted candles
you are surrounded by or the man who places his hands upon you so
that you murmur uh-huh uh-huh as I try to tell you that I am with
you in this place.

You are on fire and are the fire, lady,
at the same time that you rise twirling into the sky.
You are a campfire we built of driftwood on the beach,
and the ocean is moving in upon you without thought.
You are that fire, and yet, as evening draws deeper
you sit in front of your television set or computer net-
work is the alluring of us all, and is the heat that sends us up.

It is so hard to know
as each ember rises into the night,
whether it transfigures from the logs that give it birth

or from the gnats that with evening rise toward destiny.
The music of the waves are the same whichever way it goes.
We are a slow turtle dragging our bellies across the sand
to lay eggs in an environment so harsh we cannot long survive.

The embers rise on warmth or catch the currents where wind blows.
A lightening bug flickers green in the grass, an invitation to eternity.

Driving Small Town America

what is it to play michaelangelo's adam
        and reach out a sistine finger
                to   BOMB
with a fingertip
        when nothing comes back at you?

Look to the video arcades of the service economy:
America is only days away from waging war in Iraq;
I paint with blood, and it is not recognized as blood, though
your work, America, has folded up with the streets of backhill towns
and your police force and your teachers and your firemen have boarded planes
that scrape the edge of night from your pallet and lay it deep

nobody counts the fish killed
by a rock falling out of another universe

in Mendota, LeMoille, Princeton, Galesburg, Macomb, and Lewiston;
in every little Illinois town and cluster of slatty shacks collapsed in between,
the streets are empty of strollers, shoppers, lovers;
the cafes are closing down
the town renovation and revitalization programs running down,
the nightlife non-existent even the cruising of small town malls is gone.

If you make atoms behave like they behave in the beginning
when it is not the beginning
they will make a beginning that is like the birth of the universe

This is how Historic Americana along the 1950s gateways to tomorrow is playing out
                                    STILL/SILENT
around barren courthouse squares in the spring of two thousand and three
there are no newspapers that tell readers what is going on in Washington or the world

or that have for christ's sake more than a few pages on the local issues
and who is doing what or marrying whom
there are no news stations on the radio or television that provide perspective
if there can be any perspective
between the peeling rust of infrastructure we drive along inevitably
and the markers by the courthouses listing those who died in World Wars I and II:
64 names listed in granite in towns with no more than 200 families now—
as if some gigantic force had sucked all the vitality out of our past
and we have not yet caught up.

In the beginning is the word
and it is   BOMB

Evening Along The Outer Banks

Because we are endless in our separation
    because in our separation we are infinitely far from each other
        because the shadows on the cave wall are insubstantial and have no depth
            because we are by necessity one in our infinite separation
and the illusion is as permeable as limestone carved by rain
    and the limestone is formed from infinite forms become one
        and is washed away
          and the shadows play upon its wall,
we wander these streets without direction
    and the broken street lamps are shaped in metals factories ignited deep
beneath the earth to burn dark upon our commerce and molded
    all to be the same,
facing up different streets and destinies laid out upon a grid.

Because we are tossing within our bodies,
    carrying within our minds,
        are tossing within our minds are our bodies
swept as through kelp beds off familiar shores
    our skin smooth against each other in creating or destroying
and steeped in our sweat
we swim caught in this fabric we spin
        because
to reach out is to reach within ourselves and to breathe
is to take in what is outside and make ourselves anew,
we are spinning our skins from dry reeds on forgotten riverbanks
and are spinning our skins from the infertile roots of cotton plants on dying land
and are spinning our skins from polyester strands of fossil ferns
      in our reaching out
are the meshes we cannot reach through but through our weaving
from the abstract to the physical to the abstract
    there are the kelp and marsh grasses growing

                    -the universes between them!-
and the cottons and the polyester polystyrenes we whisper into
become the disks and the clothes and the words we wear
swimming outward through the mesh we weave
          in seeking words we reach into the ether
                    finding shadows on the limestone
disks we carry from computer to computer in our pockets,
rocketing into the dark each night from our interweb homes
          each day from our interwebbed offices leaving tracks
                    traceable each to each along the hollow streets
we seek what is within us each.

Because our portals are our eyes
          because our portals are our mouths
                    because our portals are our lungs that bring the world within us
and our lungs drive our thoughts and drive our fingers
                    because, some say, our thumbs are opposed,
we build cell-like structure to match the meshes we create
because to create, we must take a moment to ourselves within the night together
because we enter the world through each others' portals
and our beginnings are our endings.

An Erosion

Dark rivers which are not there
separate the grains of earth and roll
out among the particles which form our eastern glacial plains;
waters channeled from rains which do not come from here
quietly collected while no one looks
packaging themselves in cement and metal pipeways
circumventing/going under everything we are;
the great fishes which slide with the speed and stillness of thought
filling their dimensions.
Under highways and the flat pavement of apartment office buildings
they are descending devoid of thinking things,
carriers of dying specimens of vegetation,
they roll out in greater speed and volume
  until they pass in one black leap upon the oceans.

And there where it comes to the surface...
He's sitting there turning your white belly in his mind
as it tumbles end over hairless end
somewhere where the artesian well brings it all
  to the surface
tumbling it through his work worn fingers...

...He stands there thumbs
knitted through his belt
or he squats there leering into the space before him,
but whatever/whoever/however he stands,
it is through the lean tiredness
he extends from beneath his brows
and reaching out caresses the earth with

so when he laughs

as he does now
when first thinking he is seeing
   your limbs flash
like distant fish...
and then again when he knows that they are not...
But he stands there
and he stands there.
The lights come on in factories along the shore
and in restaurants and he
watches the one wave disappearing into the next
and waits the wait of the fisherman...

leaning back, he flips a silver
         med
   al
     li
       on
   high
into the air above him where
it turns glittering inscription over inscription
in tight descending circles beneath the clouds.
He smiles as it traces through the trees.

Offshore a white bird rises from the waves
and dips into evening.

Picking Up The Empty Packages

I have seen summer flicker in the flash of your legs running across evening lawns,
and have sought comfort in cold beers and hot charcoal grills,
in bluefish pulled from the cold Atlantic darkness charring with garlic sauce;
in laughter on aging wooden porches left behind by other families,
gazing beyond you and beyond the fences toward where crickets sing.

I am heavy as the night as I pile empty boxes and styrofoam popcorn into plastic bags.
I wish that I could know that these are indeed only the empty husks,
the precious packaging that held meaning in…
but regardless it goes out now into mustiness and trucks and then the earth…
the Christmases and birthdays we have shared and put away.

I will keep the cards, hand-drawn or store-bought,
with their simple words and line-drawings
that go on forever into my brain.

Erie

The far side of Erie
moves against our continent behind strong winds,
eating its way into shallow inlets,
cascading between countries.
On the far side, metal buckets capture what is lost from trees,
boiling it down to be sold to Americans.
Summer houses huddle in box green door frames,
hanging from their shutters along dirt roads.

Louisiana jazz man carries his battered horn
into the swampland where the moss hanging from trees
is an envelope for secret communions.
Sometimes I am sure it is the river uncovering our song.
Sometimes an owl's wings in silhouette have the shape of his lips.
Always it is raining and when you get beyond high-rise cities
paint is removed from buildings as quickly as put on.
We are far beneath the level of waves, where music plays
and undead animals occupy the shells of others' lives.

Between these,
gray stones lie in a field
outside my hometown.
I see them but cannot find my way.
I have dreamt of them each June evening
while walking from here to there and back
listening for your name in the wind.
Water is as deep as it goes.

Eyes,

what have you done with the lakeshores
I have fished along each spring among the tall grasses
speckled with goldenrod and fiery purple loosestrife,
tinged with sunset swallowtail butterflies
          hastening each to each?

Wherever you have stored this
it is inside a hollow skull. Your hollow centers tell me this,
your round portals of hope leading into despair.
Yet the halos of tiger's-eye that border you
reflect the fringes of meadows that are always with you.

Why have I carried these vacant spaces with me
to fill them and carry them on mile beyond year if only to leave them here,
having no bottom and containing nothing or everything?
Why have you swept the horizons and stared into star filled nights
and sought the inky darkness of words on pages written by the dead
if you are going to filter them into a bony bowl to be left behind?

Talking To My Son

I want you to remember this:
how city stone in evening softens,
how, like limestone, the heaviness settles,
how what was meant gathers in caverns
sweating with the coolness of patience;
I want you to remember how translucent the stone
was in its reaching out, how
you were not sure where its boundaries ended.

I want you to remember
evening people are not the same as day;
that because they are fewer they are important
as the gray space settling between lamps;
that their forcefields are cut sharp
as the crystal you drink from,
and their power to produce change uncertain,
since little happens in the city night
that has not happened before,
but when it does it is beyond control;
that there is no direct association
between a woman's words
and your love.

Having Passed The Solstice

At the end of June, the country is dying,
shriveling its skin. People are going on through nothing,
televisionadscarsbythebumpercroploadbursting out of new car lots,
seeingweaponsofmassdestructiontoo in malls,
we reflect like a polished kitchen table by candlelight used to do.

The drought is severe this year.
Grasslands in the Great Plains suburbs are in flame,
and a culture that has no belongings to cast a shadow cannot stand.
The sea comes in to claim its own at last inch by inch and year by year,
as millennia ago, but as then it is a sea of salt where little holds.

A man tends what a man can tend and disregards the rest.
I have buried the parent generation of my family on both sides
before and after the Trade Towers fell and before Al Qaeda was a base or a deception.
The trees around our little plot of land have been cut back from our lot in life
without knowing in their slow growing hearts and heavy trunks the world has changed,
but the drought is severe this year and a man must do what a man can do and leave the rest.

There's a symptomatic breaking down, I think,
that has nothing to do with guns or renegades but with the seed of man
and what happens when it shrivels like a weed from too much feeding in bad ground.
There's not much pretty about weeds breaking through the bricks on dust locked lots
with their thread hair roots pushed above ground trying to steal water from the sun—
shallow roots open to an earth bright by day and a universe black beyond black beyond.
All that weed can do is put out acid from those roots and break more down to find the
   earth it came from.

Sometimes there comes a rain. Sometimes the roots take hold,
dig their way down into a softer soil formed from the things that lived before.
But they never believe even in a wordless way that "That's enough. That will hold."
They will always grow beyond the resources they have formed,
great leafy vegetation that knocks down houses and institutions when the year is good.

Imagination And The Man

A falcon landed in the apple tree outside my window yesterday:
a bird of the sky and high telephone poles, that would not act like this.
Yet he sat there, focusing the small twigs and leaves around him,
drawing the whole vast structure of the tree into his intensity.
Until in the end there was nothing but his eye that I was looking at;
all else moved around it as fog moves across a meadow.
I sat on the sofa facing him, not six feet and one pane of glass away,

It would be foolish to say I think that we were matched
or that we were bound together, but it is true that time binds and we were there.
Had either of us moved, the surface would have broken, mirrors shattered.
It was a touch of magic in my home, empty of people and filled with life.
And then it spread its wings, tangled briefly in the tightly wound limbs,
and was gone. I will not sleep tonight, nor for many more.

It Is Time

It is time.
Your hand reaches out and punches the button.

It is time.
Each morning the slab of your hand clamps down.

It is time.
To get up and drop your suit on your back and eat toast.

Every morning
It is the same time

And every morning we go out
to the same meadows where you hunted yesterday
and it is the same time
and you stalk the same kind of game.

It takes time we do not know for a field to regenerate itself.
It takes time outside of a watch for a stream to flow clean with the swift gills of fish.
But every morning when the hunt goes out, we go out to the same field
picked so barren by now that the only game to eat is ourselves.
This heart that we keep clutched to our chests, eating hunched over at the end of day,
is stocked there by common taxes, and is bitter, and is our own.

It is time
by another meaning in the dark soil above tundra line,
every morning when your hand clamps down on what is important,
there are very *unimportant* flowers close as our mountains,
paper thin whites and blues and yellows smaller than postage stamps,

brief as six weeks of winter in the sunshine days of August,
farther than a roadmap of our cities,
with petals rising one maybe two inches above the frozen soil
and roots reaching down five feet *pushing five feet* into the ice
each morning when your hand says it is time…
they are frozen into winter and into the rock soil beneath them,
but with their roots flexible even through the ice to twist aside from the rocks that surge
      beneath them.
From rocks that break loose from bedrock it is so cold,
heaving and rising through the soil like leviathans the size of school buses,
because of the buckling, creaking soil down where summer's heat does not go,
they smash their way up, even like your hand coming down on time.
And the unimportant flowers, still unthinking, shift their roots to escape severing.
There are the lichens also unlike to you who live their lives on the bare rock of their
      necessity
so slowly but inevitably each lichen itself can live two thousand years.

      It is time
      but each morning your hand comes down
      and your body gets up for the feeding ground
at the same time even these rocks themselves rise from the ground
and silver thin root fingers swirl paste them into the darkness of earth-time.

Reflecting On The Visions

If I were Pablo Van Gogh
and were to go to a window, and looking out, say
I see a multi-faceted tower of lights that moves when I move
and the sun gets in my eyes so that I squint and see bright swathes of color,
would I know if the far side of the window were backed with silver
and the gyrations of the tower were gusts of wind slamming against that thin sheet, or
would I know that slumping red and brown Monet beasts hunched down in fields,
and would I hurry to take their sketches as I imagined them;
or would I look at that flat misshapen beast slouching toward me
and say this is me because I recognize the ravages of war?

Would I hear John Cage playing in the music from a farther room?
And in such confusion, what would I tell you then, or where would I lean,
when I do not know the color of my eyes or shape of my limbs?
The photographs I have seen are of an old fat man with flappy hands,
not the lone wolf who streaks through silent streets at night.

I shall be Hamlet listening for rats behind the curtains,
and their toenails ticking on the castle floors will be the minute hands of clocks;
I will put them in a shining metal case and wear it on a chain beneath my vest
for important evening parties, for the white haired Albert Einstein scribbling on a board.
If I were to go to the window again and again and again, I would take you all
and write that my name is Henry David Thorough and I will simplify,
and either I will miss it all or take it in.

The Lessons Of Millennia

We learned that in the midst of ourselves we were most alone.
The best among us would sit in rooms filled with books of the dead.
The worst among us also, for that is where the words were written,
and the beginning was the word.
We learned that it was written in many languages and meant many things,
that it sent men into the spaces between stars or destroyed them,
that it was memory from one race of people to the next, from one
long dead pioneer to the young descendent writings letters to her son
across a continent sitting in his room listening to rain fall outside his walls.
There was not much else, though we gave degrees for this,
and we changed the word; oh, we wrote whole technologies, whole analogies
and learned infinite separation of the inseparable in all detail.

What it came down to, though,
was I liked to have a drink in the evening...
drank of the grasses that grew golden on distant meadows
drawing into the hidden words of my own world,
having bought them on labeled bottles in the marketplace.
And the marketplace was the same for every one of us who bought,
whether Plato or Caesar or Mr. Jones,
whatever the choices was it really so different for any one of us then
when we drank the draught that brought us all together once again?

So Much Growing

Something to count the days by
       Red-hued husks from a dogwood
          Wind that issues seasons in

Our peach tree blooms in northern Illinois
having produced one swollen vulva in its life
which we sucked dry as the stone it grows from,
still specially sweet in its landscaped swirl of Bradford pears, flowering
    plum, magnolia cadence
working the soil for memories

Ducks brooding in the flower bed on Easter
       beneath pines where magenta straw flowers grow
          so much growing at the edge of the great plains!

Doktor will see you now
something in your tummy yum yum
is eating its way out as despair or as tomorrow.
The last thing anyone will want to see of you
is the last thing they will ever see and will bury deep.
I do not want to think of ejaculations between bone
and yet in that blank socket lies
all the eyes you have seen and lips touched.

Tossing Jobs Around Like Manhole Covers

Between places that belong to other people
   there is no money.
            I think I will sell cars.
I will link data bases to windows.
I will look inside them and pick gaudy ornaments
that reflect the light of old movies.

Everyone is a clearing in the snow;
            a coming in;
                     a vacuum.
Leaves that shaded us last spring
are brown bodies swirled across fields.
They are gathered in by our industry
                     and it is silent.
We are waiting for someone to live.

A sound
            would make the air vibrate.
The cold would shatter, cascading to the floor.
      There would be
            a floor.

Within The Islands Of Solitude

This season as the death chill grows upon us and our seeds are carefully stored,
wind shutters about us like a cat worries a raccoon. Tentative because
it might catch hold of what it's up against, but of course, wind isn't a thinking thing.
Wind is that which passes over all else, shudders dimly in the back of consciousness,
grabs hold of worm-worn wooden storage sheds filled with what we seek to hold
and hurls their boards apart to reveal the emptiness kept inside.

But the wind, the passing wave of change, is not itself what comes inside,
not when all the photographs and recipes and matchbooks have been stored
and been burst apart in immense conflagrations that the scope of time cannot hold.
These are dull thoughts in a dry land, but will not be eroded because
like granite beneath the fields, they lie beneath inhuman consciousness
tearing apart the bedrock that supports each green young thing,

A case in point: Achilles' armor washed in red, a battered thing
which life had emptied out of, leaving the empty space of a blind man's eyes inside
to describe those things beyond the scope of human consciousness,
to find words for the winds that carried ships of wisdom stored
and lost in seas that were crushed between jagged rocks, seas crushed because
even the water that fills our thoughts, that is our thoughts, cannot hold.

What then, if we could set our own sails anew might we seek to hold
beyond the goatskin saddlebags we carry and each rusted metal thing
we bring home to lay upon the necks of our children, who snicker because
we have got it wrong, they know; we have it wrong deep inside…
know somehow the grains we carefully selected, fermented, and stored,
are lost to our words, and with each draught distort our consciousness.

Blind men always are the greatest singers of inhuman consciousness
bringing forth the greatest dreams of men, dreams of the skull and what it can hold,
dreams of the ocean and continents beyond, of the sky and all that can't be stored

in cylindrical metered pipettes on lab benches, with each labeled thing a thing
that is unlike anything else there is when you get to the blankness deep inside.
Blind men are the heavy hitters in this, with their far fetched imagery because

there is an emptiness that fills all water and the eyes of men, and because
water itself erodes all things and is filled itself with all things. Consciousness
among the other dragons, sculptures, *piano fortissimos* whirled about inside
wraps about itself in the vast oceans of space that lie about us and grabs hold
of the sun, the moon, a young girl's legs, of any image that can make this thing,
this goatskin bag we call ourselves worthy of being words, of thoughts that can be stored.

Because in the distance of time, wind isn't a thinking thing we seek to hold,
consciousness cannot be measured. In the traverse of our lives there is no thinking thing
inside the wind that distorts and shaves and spreads apart all things before they're stored.

Witnessing the writer who tried to raise a family; dark matter at the beginning of the 21st century

We could have done so much
had we not been waylaid by electronic screens,
thinking data was information;
thinking information was our job.

Thinking back, when I met you, I laughed
not because your cashmere sweater was one of Lot 345026
but because your timidly hopeful fingers had touched it,
so that when you put it over your young flesh you hoped
you would be something more refined or romantic than you are.
I knew then that that was impossible. I knew
something I have forgotten through the years,
and through the years we could have done so much

for you
and the tendrils of civilization
you plucked without knowing anything,
but believing that there was something worth it all in me…
and I, believing we knew everything,
stayed awake at night, not thinking about colleges or food or bills
but you

and out of that for all these years
as we have searched each other's needs across the country
turn forward the clock

take a man with a high level of education
who has learned to live among and serve those who have wealth
and has learned to generate capital in excess of expenditures
in a job that he has served for the primary benefit of those around him

                    --the public good--
through the sun sere years when he thought he could *make a difference in the world,*
and through the years when the icon of innocent wife and children had a claim,
and let him be smart enough in his own skin that he does not put his life on credit,
and then and only then deprive him of his job through downsizing
when he is still young and in good health, and he will still
be bored
pursue sex
tear at the fabric of society
be dangerous to other men who are raising families, and if he is a poet
do something about it.
He may rape, riot, kill, or just do crossword puzzles as befits his nature.
He will be unhappy until someone wiser gives him destiny
or someone younger makes him young.
You cannot kill the onus of learning when you let it out of the jar;
you younger fellows take note, you bureaucrats and social engineers
take note lest ye be paid in ways you did not dream.

Gray suits gray
          landscapes clothes for the silent shark gliding
  his way around the coral landscapes. The shark draws no attention;
matches his environment silently;
manipulates the clown fish bright in their orange and white scarves
  bright colors that signal sexual attraction media coverage sales of gum snapping jeans
  leaders of populist votes that get out the army and drive the guns across continents and
  oceans
without their even being aware as one then another twitches slightly to the right
looking exuberant come get me get me I'm the one;
he eats when he is hungry and is invisible when he is not;
he lives in wall street washington and the east coast corridors,

endangered gray, but muted
as the land is muted in all its colorations
forming patterns that merge into a star white light upon blackness,
one of many too many to be counted.
A society of arrogance and assurance,
but *la via del tren subterraneo es pelagrosa.*
Our gods are more of swan than of Aries,
though they do not act the part;
more of Aristophanes than of Euripides.
Proud Ilium, you have fallen so long ago you are in shards
described only in the words of a blind man
who saw the darkness of armor clattering around him
rather than the shadows of republic on the wall.

This is as things are after increasingly knowing everything for two thousand years.
We have eyes that we might perceive those things that give off light.
We have ears that we might perceive those things that give off sound.
We have writing that we might perceive those things that are dark matter
and make up all that we cannot see or hear, and that is by far the greater part:
it is a moot point. All things expand from the moot point by inverse ratio.

Somebody's got to pick up,
has to make the time to sort the days,
find out what happened between purchases from the store
             that are already stored on data discs for further purchasing indicators
                       sweating the little things
someone has to judge the blank patterns because
that's what holds us together on the bank of Walden Pond
                       not the purchases that are known
with our twenty-three rows of pea plants that someone somewhere stored away,
or to think about the things that were never written down about each blade of grass

           between them,
some bum who has no need to be told or sold the little things.

Does this have meaning,
that *en vino es veritas*, and we have come so far from our homes
to meet in a bottle before a candle in a dark paneled room in a sophisticated mating dance
that we don't rut and sleep,
that I have stayed awake so many nights
thinking I wanted nothing but to lie in a field beneath the stars
    listening to crickets
           loved and loving in the eternal youth of animals
                killed and killing without thought
except that there were children who wanted these things as well,
and since I hadn't gotten them maybe then they…
does this have meaning when you put on your sassy spring outfit
and go to town after so many days are gone.
Somebody has to take the time to think it through.

When All Is Said

Private First Class Williamson floats in a small rubber boat
on a wide and blank sea
feeling the swells of the ocean lifting him
      sliding sideways
            pushing against his flesh
  and circling
as though something powerful were holding him
to take him somewhere with a secret purpose.
The swells ripple at his fingertips and swirl his belly deep above
      some dark emptiness.
The sky is the horizon, and he is gray with evening.

He shoots his last flare high into an endless mist,
where magnesium roars into a statement of experience.
He is alone, cannot drink the water, cannot reach out any further,
is afraid that something powerful moves beneath him implacable.
He has circled the constellations, he finds, as darkness rises.

Again he fires his last flare in memory,
              and it is a star;
    and the stars reach out with all their raging energy to answer him,
      and the arms of his lost companions far below reach upward
  as thirst fills his throat until his tongue blackens in his mouth.

He drinks from the waters, and the thirst fills his mind beneath the stars.
He is rocked with the blood of the lamb in his dreams.

When It's Time To Go

When you have done what you can do,
    when you have been thanked
and are standing with your back to an open stairway
and a stone courtyard of tradition surrounds you
    in all directions
        sometimes
            you go inside
                and listen
                    to the walls.
They vibrate with madness
that is so dense it cannot scream.
It cannot flake off like the paint in your home.
It was quarried deep beneath the earth
    where it is dark
        and light comes only
            with a chisel
                or dynamite
                    and is everlasting
except that some part of the stone retains darkness
and holds it deep within its heart
    while the boot soles of other hearts bounce off.
You wander there
    after the thanks
        and you go home.

Trout Fishing Along The Alagash

A trout moves up into moonlight
and sucks life from the surface of his pool.
The life knows of nothing larger below it,
but is gone before it is aware of life.
Each day, year beyond year, the river dimples.
We are folded into our desks, ears clamped to a wire,
fingers tapping tabulations.

A Space Between Time

In the first three months, her new car
has measured out 1595 miles
of rain swept black roads that I am unaware of. I can read
the numbers. I can see
the wheels, and feel their heavy erasers passing over us.

There is a space I do not know how to fill,
inhabited by fear soaked suits waiting to be worn again.
These suits have flown about the country to speak in meeting halls
so many times they have nothing to fear from missing miles.
They carry the junk of hotel rooms in their pockets.
They carry the words of twenty five years lived alone.
I can enumerate
the deals. I can taste the cocktail glitter;
the meals. I can read what I have failed to do each day.

Things To Remember

(A Protagonist Poem In Nine Parts)

1.

The smoke detection device hanging by the kitchen
contains Radioactive Elements
    according to the label
and may someday save your life.
If it cracks or must be disposed of,
  you are ordered to send it to the factory.
Someone in your family must package it.

2.

All things are alive.
The gas storage tank ½ mile away is waiting
    for the perfect moment.

3.

You are not holding the wheel
as your wife or husband drives to work.
You are not even in the car.

4.

Sometimes you will think
you recognize a coat sleeve or a hat
passing out of reach in the corner of a crowd.
Sometimes it will follow you.

5.

The Christ child may even now
be leafing through a book of verse
    and reading Yeats.

6.
Oranges are sometimes green.

7.
If you walk to work
you will save yourself the cab fare.
Every taxi driver approaching the intersection
   is aware of that.
He wants to earn a living too.
There are six intersections to be crossed
   each morning.
He has twelve times to reach a decision each day.

8.
The can of mushroom soup
is three years old today
and is dented deeply on both sides.
It is the last can on the shelf.

9.
The sun is shining more days than not
somewhere throughout the world.

Of Moons

In the worlds of the pigeon
lying as wax below the airconditioner,
the air does not smell of birds;
there is no reason to walk through old feathers
   upon the ground.

I stretch the sun like a needle
        through the turrets of an old church in the Bowery
where glass bottle ships unhinge their sails;
this is tomorrow   in its only form
and seeds crackle like slingshots under feet.

Sweet Mother of the western plains,
   your son is forgotten where the crows eat out his liver
      in sweating bars   in the Great City,
the city of the plastic trees and artificial dustmops.
He does not speak your language any longer,
   building signal fires from aluminum canoes.
He cannot swim the mighty Hudson or Potomac or Mississippi
   in order to reach out to you;
he would be lost upon the Colorado, although he pays paths to lose him more.
Your stone teeth are almost forgotten in the sudden quiet
of a farmer eating peaches in an Alaskan spring.

A pool of coins
sits under candlelight,
the object of attention
in a quiet room.
Men roll up their sleeves and curse
as sweat rolls down their hands.
The windows are vacant.

A pigeon tours beneath the clouds
in a vacuum
between stones and air,
and is hated from both sides—
a meal or a leaver of debris.
Its eyes are painted barns from Pennsylvania Dutch
and it walks among craters of the moon.
The year is early, and wings make hollow noises in the streets.

Returning Home

Four years have gone by
     and the girls have moved away   married
     one gone mad in prison
and he sits invisible in his suit
  in the village gathering place
  untouched…
all those things that he would never be.
But he is home, and the leaves have left the trees.

He sits at the table he always sat at—
the enemy of the juke box banter
  he has learned to disbelieve
because it makes the money he now makes and does not trust,
and runs away on steel guitars into the hills
like the wild eyes of animals caged too long.
The bartender knows them all and watches him beneath raised eyebrows
  and does not drink.

Say that time is a hollow sieve which has no holes
and which drags about each ankle he places on the floor;
that it fills the creases of his coat as he puts it on;
that you always have to put it on
     and there is no death or motion…
and he will follow you home, old friend,
and speak of all those things that you will never say.
Quietly, as the DVD in the walls,
  he will leave you to sleep;
and when you wake, his coat will be hung across your chair.

Coming Of Age

The lantern lights on the screen make you unaware.
You focus on them and their dim halos,
but the while walls are your incubator and albumen.
They are Mother Hen, Mother Media, Mother Medea,
and your own wing flaps are scarce heard
tucked into your body and clipped off as they are.

It is written in the band about your ankle,
registered in the game warden's book for your collector.

When we made the Pullman cars, it was to pull men.
When we made the Pullman towns, it was to pool them.
When we made Carnegie mills and Model Ts, we built a caravansary.
When we built computers, we computed men. And then
when we built the Internet, we commuted them.
When we let the people in,
we let them pay the bill at the gates of moral bankruptcy,
and nailed them on Christmas messiah trees,
became cubicles watching walls across America
while America was watching us outsourcing prophecies.

Long life! Long productivity! Drink the drink.
Enhance life with the dance of lights
and we pull the mind of men apart again,
running ever faster to our smaller spaces
inside white painted rooms with airtight seals.
The warden waits to check us in.

The Last Snow Fell

I have stayed out in the snow a long time.
The wind blew it round beneath the street lamps
until they were turned to plaques of marble in the trees.
It is easier to understand everything when I am not by your side;
I stayed beneath the big tree in the meadow across from your home,
as you turned the house lights off and passed from room to room.
I stayed as the roads grew invisible and silent and wide.
I stayed, remembering what we planned to do and see

when we were still talking to each other and had plans
to share our memories only with each other; it was a long time.
The snow fell, laying blankets over me, turning the ground cold.
My bones were cold, my eyes dark, my flesh stretched parchment.
You will never know I did not mean to leave you to grow old;
nor to leave us apart forever that evening when I went.

Hollowman

Hollowman has no ears...
the bones in his head tremble.

Nothing yet registers
the bonework latticed beneath metal
or that Hollowman has gone,
has swept as smoke through the windows of his own skull;
his metal liquefies itself tirelessly
slowly filling Prism
eating at walls
until holes begin to curl their lips back
and the entire structure then
                            collapses
in acrid smoke of seething flesh.

Nothing then fills his veins
unformed perfect his mind
since nothing had come before
save shells singing their hollow oceans
    into time...

So, Here's Then To The People

So, here's then to the people who care:
who don't huddle in the dark cold corners of the city
but though screamed at by the wolves of money each day
can come back for one more round the next
or leave it alone if they want.

Here's to the children who believe
women and children are children and live forever
though childhood passes from them themselves
like the ballgame with its perennial nine players
and go singing discovery forever into their hands.

Here's to the man who wears a gray suit
so that the twisted, scarred metal of his sides is hidden
so that his entrails can be contained to protect family:
to the man who wants his sons and daughters to know country air,
who wants them to sing the songs of sirens;
who in beating his brain out through the back of his skull
finds escape in the oceans beyond thought.

Here's to the woman who learns Business
thinking to match friendship with the boys she knew,
but finds mannequins in the aisles of fairy tales;
to the people who never had poetry written of them
because they have given their lives for something they don't understand,
and are poetry or would be if they spoke.

Here's to the people,
Remember the people!
What about the man who forged the gun, or the man who molded
the bullet that was employed by John Wilkes Booth...or by

    the man
who killed
President Kennedy and Bobby Kennedy and Mary Joe Copechnie anyway
or the miner in the lead mine dragged down below light
to earn food in a radioactive afterglow.
Here's to the people
Remember the people!
molders of fortunes and nations,
as subtle as penicillin in a Petri dish
or the cash register…
Here's to the people
writing ballads strummed in alleys…
to the saints!

Here's to men,
for being but men
is being God,
for it is that than which nothing greater can be conceived.

Brain Creature

Brain creature comes down from the hills
snuffling light through wrinkled nostrils,
pads its way among stone tombs,
studies the fire of figurines,
howling as it breaks shadow fingers.

                    *

Windmusk calls to itself

                    *

Consciousness fills itself with the abyss of
falling trees in silent films,
leaves becoming fingers
white with cold

                    *

something begins to move inside the fragile bones of Hollowman.
Something that lies waiting in the nocturnal presence to
pull him into our time and north america filling his blood
        as a song that is history/
a song carrying other men and women in its bones...
a long drawn light exiting toward the horizon
a
bridge binding gelatin starlight to its length...
massive iron bones grinning out midnight's heat,
holding up the crush of commerce on floating pads of concrete
undulating over miles of silt washed down,
breathing life into its absence.

What fish pursue this river canyon now/
What scales tossed glittering where there is no sun?

There are no footsteps
marking their progress over stone
no wind
chilling a man's collar
no rattle to the tympany
welcoming his autumn eyes
as they open beginning the migratory sweeps of pale bray birds,
the dark crush of oceans toward equator
  and round again
a surging upward through earth gone soft.
His fingers will never come to the surface
nor will they cease pushing their way farther into the ocean
once they have left this bridge.
No one will speak his name
as they drive cars across this span.

They will earn their memories
will drive their wives to hospitals on the other side
hearing their blood pound with the wind against these girders
but they will miss this man who built their magic carpet.

Like moths
small white moths
settling their whirlwind courtship of fire
they will perish dust in dark.

                *

Birdman calls out into the gray mist surrounding him.
He sheds wings of molten candles
and cocks his head to
Infinity.
His heart fills with water
splashing its cool distance to the underground,
a memory of violence he carries within him.

                    *

Moonlaughter catches at your spine
fills the herring bone beneath your shirt.
You turn
your fingers kneading at the gray
pulling out your weight
in computer time...it goes
markachaggachagga markachaggachagga
boot soles on the intellect.

You have seen how your sun comes through
one spot in the cloud of autumn days
finding one tree burnished on your hill
isolating it in time
and memory.

You are a spindle of white
of milk drawn down by gravity
into a cupless lake of coffee
a Mississippi bayou heron tipped on eyeflesh
--a sleeter of motion beneath liquid—
drawing out concentric circles perhaps oolongs

where they brush against infringement
    then circling on again
concentricity rushing after its greater parts
but reaching down as well and warm,
folding like a mobious monster in all directions forever...
unseeable as a blank white wall
you are embedded in

your brown eyes, fawns
leaping over logs before the gun goes off
first forged from autumn's leaves,
the color of your hair
or of my mouth hanging open in its sorrow
over sand and pebbles our feet move among,
moving among the cypress knees
we leave buried in our estuaries

the shattered crystalline reflection
    --these are real substances around you dissolving!!—
a ray of sunshine in clear water,

                    *

The people carry their desks outside.
They plug their typewriters into grassy plains
            their business fax machines into the trees
                    their cell phone stock quotations into clouds
and listen to the slow call of soil,
signaling to each other how the trees respond.
Some of them take off their clothes.
Others open their collars and lie back.

This
is the peoples' choice.
It is their decision and for once
they have not forgotten the implications.
Pretty soon they get down from their swivel chairs
and smooth their hands along the ground.
Rising, they embrace.
They go off alone or in twos
listening with puzzled looks upon their faces.

       *

These are things that do not touch
      Hollowman.
He looks for a long time before disappearing into shadows.

He drops his wallet...
sleek black it wanders across fields,
gorging grass and flowers through multiple stomachs.

Motion seeps into his shell
but so slowly
that
without moving
from his case he is sailing
upright on his feet across a sky two hundred feet
above where people will turn in their fleshy machinery.

A telephone rings in his crystal,
and he of course
has no ear opening into the world

his word is gold

It is someone
some part of our future
calling to say when
it is time you will know.
You will walk the moon
searching the inside shape of self.

*

Because the earth in living could not speak
it was dead.
Because the furred animals were warm in night
and were not buildings with name tags with green water…
Because we could not imagine that stars in our own skulls
were worth the stars that our sons sought…
we could not speak,
but felt with the space between our ribs.

We go down to the rivers
filling crevices in earth
rolling where it rolls between stars
singing our sighs of molten metal
like a redwing blackbird on estuary's morning.

*

Song comes down,
tears the marrow from our spines,
separates our groins with desireless fingers,

fills our feet with shoes for walking,
casts spider webs against nova suns in dew dawn.

Song is Song,
and its caviar rattles our memories
like the fence posts of hungry fields in autumn,
our words squat pumpkins rotting into loam.

Distance,
if you think of it,
is a star immense with molten helium
in its rushing upon you upon night;
a snowflake, a star,
small indefinitely small until it settles
upon your rivers and freezes them,
bringing night wolves soft as feathers into
shadow
singing the costume jewelry of untamed talons.

About the Author

Jared Smith has a distinguished 25 year career of publication in poetry volumes and the nation's leading literary journals, while serving as a leader in continuing education and policy formation in both the public and private sectors. This includes advising the Clinton Administration on national security policy, serving as Special Appointee to Argonne National Laboratory, serving as associate director of Education and Research at a major private laboratory outside Chicago, and spearheading various private/public sector partnerships between industry and various university and government agency groups.

He has written and published poetry extensively throughout this period, as well as supporting literary development by serving executive functions in various literary organizations. Jared's poetry has appeared in *Poet Lore, The Small Press Review, The New York Quarterly, Kenyon Review, Pulpsmith, Rhino, Spoon River Quarterly, Bitter Oleander, The Pedestal, Beloit Poetry Journal, Greenfield Review, Bitterroot, Coe Review, Fine Madness, Pembroke Magazine, CrossCountry, Trail & Timberline*, and many, many others. His work has been adapted to modern dance at New York's Lincoln Center for the Performing Arts, and to musical drama at Crossroads Theatre in Naperville, Illinois. He has been interviewed and read his work on NPR radio programs. Jared is on the advisory board of *The New York Quarterly*, and Poetry Editor of *Trail & Timberline Magazine*, the official journal of the Colorado Mountain Club. He is also immediate past president of Poets & Patrons in Chicago, a member of The Chicago Poets' Club and the Illinois State Poetry Society.

Lake Michigan and Other Poems is Jared Smith's fifth book of poetry. Jared's previous books have been critically well-received by such writers as the late William Packard, Walter James Miller, Andrew Glaze, Lawrence Ferlinghetti, Harry Smith, Stanley Nelson, and others.

These books include:
Walking The Perimeters Of The Plate Glass Window Factory (2002, Birch Brook Press, NY)
Keeping The Outlaw Alive (1988, Erie Street Press, Chicago)
Dark Wing (1984, Charred Norton Publishing, NY)
and
Song Of The Blood: An Epic (1983, The Smith Press, NY)